Vegetables are for Eating

By Mr. Nibbles and
Leslie Goodale Adebonojo

Book 3 of the
Mr. Nibbles' Bites of Life
Series

Spring Knoll Press

2018

This book is a work of fiction. The character in this story, Mr. Nibbles, does not represent any other dog. Any resemblance to any other dog living or dead is entirely coincidental.

Copyright © 2018 by Leslie Adebonojo
All rights reserved.
Published in the United States.
Spring Knoll Press
ISBN 9780997874662

For Geoff

You always encouraged me to do it, so I did it again and again with pictures.

Thanks again to Katy Libby best editor ever.

Discussions and observations you may want to have with your child. This book was designed to encourage your child to create their own story using the pages without words.

Page

1   What is an animal shelter and why do dogs live there?

2-6 How do carrots grow? Why is a carrot healthy? Why is a carrot a vegetable? Why do the carrots in the grocery store come in a bag?

3   What are garden tools and how do you use them? (rack, shovel, hoe)

4   Who is a veterinarian? Why can't my pet eat my food?

9   What do you do during playtime?

13 Are sugar snap peas a vegetable? Why?

14 Do you like to eat bananas?

16 Do you like to eat blueberries? Why are they fruit?

17 How many snacks do you eat each day?

18 What is a rawhide bone made of?

For more information on how to adopt a pet contact your local animal shelter.

For more information on cooking vegetables go to "Kids in the Kitchen" Nutrition.gov

Mr. Nibbles came from a local animal shelter to live with us. He loves to run outside, sleep, play ball and chase the Moon. Vegetables are his favorite food.

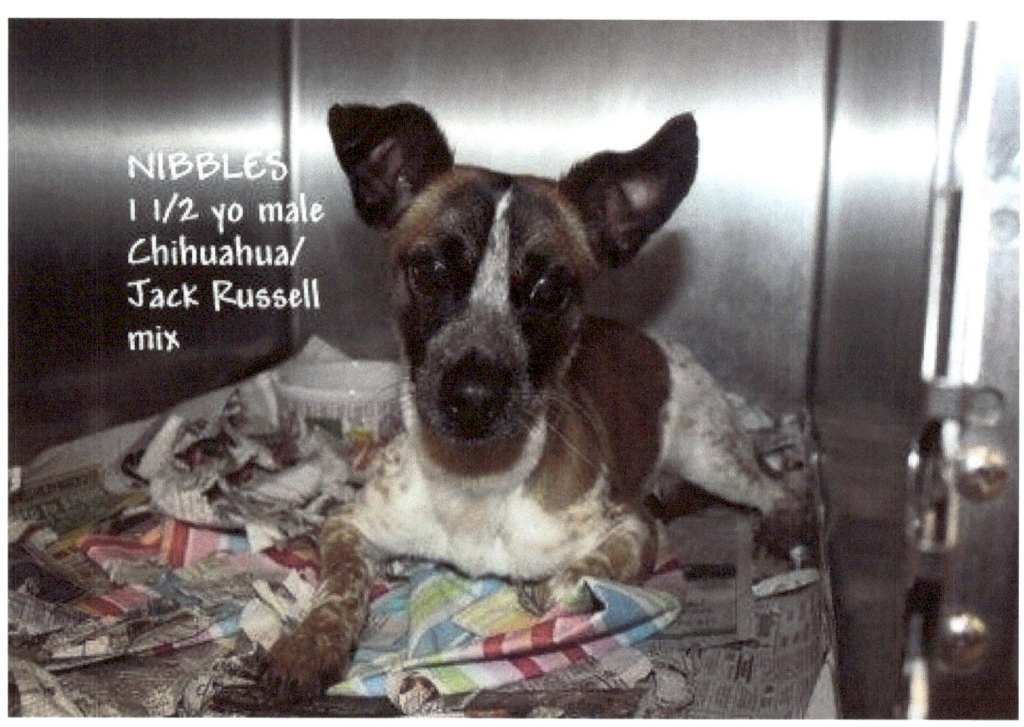

Carrots are Mr. Nibbles favorite vegetable. He doesn't like to share his carrot, so he runs outside to eat it. Can you count the carrots?

What garden tools can you see in the picture?

Be sure to check with your veterinarian before you give your pet any food other than the food made especially for them.

I use my paws so the carrot won't run away.

Mr. Nibbles sits by the refrigerator because that's where the carrots come from.

Playtime!

Is this a snack?

Mr. Nibbles likes cooked green beans. Can you count the green beans in his bowl?

He even likes green beans with his dinner. Can you count the green beans?

These are sugar snap peas. Can you count the peas in their shell?

Next on the snack menu is some fruit. Your veterinarian will tell you how many snacks your pet may eat each day.

Can you count the banana pieces that Mr. Nibbles eats for his snack?

How many blueberries will Mr. Nibbles eat? Do you like to eat blueberries?

Mr. Nibbles never eats more than one snack a day even though he might want another one.

Apples are great too!

Sometimes a rawhide bone is fun to chew on.

Naptime please.

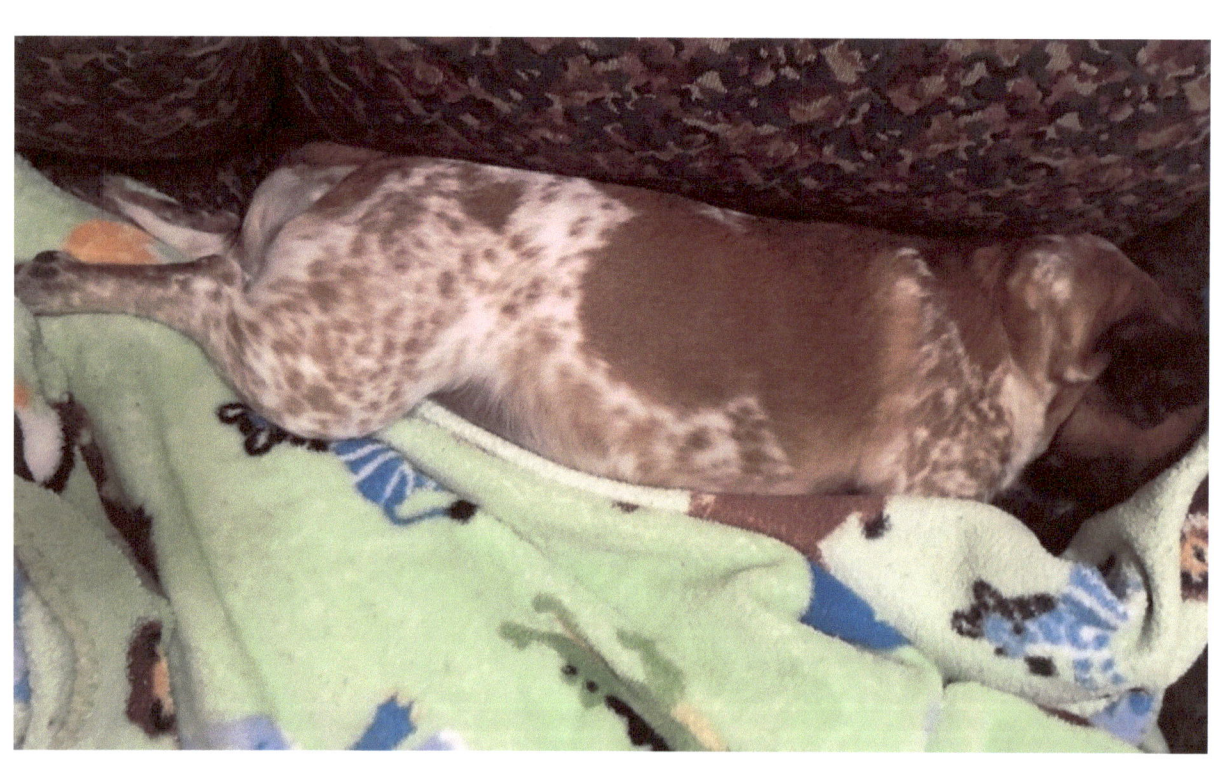

Up from his nap and ready to go, again. Bye, Bye.